Original title:
Peachy Delights

Copyright © 2025 Creative Arts Management OÜ
All rights reserved.

Author: Jasper Montgomery
ISBN HARDBACK: 978-1-80586-423-3
ISBN PAPERBACK: 978-1-80586-895-8

Sweet Summer Serenade

In a land where fruits do giggle,
The juiciest tease makes folks wiggle.
Bright hues dancing in the heat,
Who knew snacks could be so sweet?

Bouncing bites in every bowl,
Sticky fingers take their toll.
Laughter spills with every crunch,
Snack attacks, a perfect brunch!

Juicy Dreams

Slippery skins that tease the tongue,
In sunny patches, songs are sung.
With every squirt, a burst of glee,
Join the fruit parade, oh me!

Daydreams float like fruity stew,
Riding clouds in shades of blue.
Life's a whirl of juicy fun,
Let's all party 'til we're done!

Golden Sunlit Bites

Bite into sunshine, oh what a thrill,
Crispy sweetness, such a skill.
Juicy laughter flows around,
With each slice, joy can be found.

Wobbling squirrels join the feast,
A fruit buffet, to say the least.
Golden hues paint skies above,
Making memories, hearts will shove!

Nectar's Kiss

Whispers of flavor, a sweet surprise,
A nectar fountain, oh how it flies.
Sipping nectar like it's wine,
Every drop divine and fine.

Bubble over with fruity cheer,
Gather 'round, let's all draw near.
With sticky cheeks and happy grins,
This fruity party just begins!

Nature's Sweet Embrace

In the orchard, fruits collide,
A dance of flavors, side by side.
Bouncy smiles, from tree to tree,
Swinging low, as happy as can be.

Branches giggle in the breeze,
Bees buzz round with swarming ease.
Each bite bursts with laughter sweet,
Nature's joke, a juicy treat.

The Golden Hour Droplet

Sunset drips like honey gold,
Liquid laughter, stories told.
Clouds wear aprons, dusk a chef,
Chopping sunlight with a laugh, oh yes!

A splash of joy on grassy blades,
Nature's pranks in warm cascades.
Sipping colors, oh so bright,
While crickets play under the night.

A Dance of Juices

Drippy fun on summer days,
Squirrels play in fragrant rays.
Twists and turns of citrus beams,
As nature giggles, bursting seams.

Slurpy sounds on slippery ground,
Juicy jokes all around.
With each drop, a playful tease,
Tickling tongues with sticky breeze.

Sunlit Charms

Lighthearted smiles as shadows play,
Fruits sing songs of summer's sway.
A radiant grin from the sun above,
Sharing warmth, it's pure fruit love.

Bubbly laughter from trees so tall,
Nature's party, come one, come all!
With every glance, there's joy to find,
In this orchard of the silly kind.

Orchard Reverie: A Taste of Joy

In the orchard, laughter flies,
Fruit like smiles in sunny skies.
Wobbling on the branches high,
One fell down—thought it could fly!

Juicy treats in every bite,
Tickling tongues, what pure delight!
Nature's giggle, sweet and round,
Bouncing laughter all around.

Wistful Memories Beneath the Boughs

Underneath the boughs we'd play,
Chasing critters, bright and gay.
Who knew fruit could cause such glee?
Caught a squirrel—Oh, wait! That's me!

Sticky fingers, carefree days,
Eating fruit in silly ways.
Laughter echoes, seeds to spit,
The joy of age cannot outwit.

Celestial Shades of Fruitful Elegance

Orbs of color, hanging low,
Moonlit dance, what a show!
Each one sings a silly song,
Plump and ripe, they get along.

In the dusk, we laugh and muse,
Ballet steps with juicy booze.
Nature's punchline, sweetly bold,
This fruity tale will never grow old.

Sunwoven Dreams of a Perfect Day

Sunrise whispers, bright and warm,
Orchard chimes in playful swarm.
Fruit fights flying through the air,
Dodging bites with joyful flair!

Every snack a chance to tease,
Juicy giggles in the breeze.
Nature's jesters, oh so sweet,
One last laugh before we eat!

Warm Skin and Soft Fruit

Under the sun, we laugh and play,
Juicy treasures roll away.
Sticky fingers, silly grins,
Chasing sweetness, where it begins.

A splash of juice, a squishy mess,
Warming hearts, we must confess.
The squirrels envy our sweet feast,
Nature smiles, its antics unleashed.

A Taste of Innocence

With every bite, we giggle loud,
Innocence wrapped in a fruity cloud.
The world is bright, so sweet and round,
Childlike wonders all around.

Laughter spills like golden juice,
Moments like these, we can't refuse.
Even bees buzz in delight,
Casting shadows, light and bright.

Embrace of the Orchard

In the orchard, we roam free,
Hopping around like we're on spree.
Branches bow under heavy load,
Nature's jokes are quite the code.

A comical twist by a friendly tree,
Whispering secrets just for me.
As I tumble, laugh, and spin,
Soft fruits giggle, let the fun begin!

Ripened Revelations

Each bite unveils a cheeky tease,
With every laugh, the heart finds ease.
Bright colors dazzle, playful sights,
Turning wrong turns into delights.

A roll here, a slip there too,
Nature's chaos in the view.
Ripeness brings a hearty chuckle,
Jolly moments, life's sweet shuffle.

Sugary Serenade

In a garden where giggles grow,
A fruit that's pink puts on a show.
It wiggles and jigs with every bite,
Sweetness bursts, it's pure delight.

Juicy treasure in a fuzzy coat,
Eating it makes me dance and gloat.
I drip and drool, what a sight,
Ripe jokes slip through, oh what a plight!

Rolling around like a ball of joy,
Yellow and red, oh what a ploy.
It teases my taste with each big munch,
Who knew fruit could be such a punch?

So grab a fork or just dive in,
With laughter, we'll feast, we'll surely win.
Fruity fun for all to share,
Come take a bite, if you dare!

Whitespace of Fruit

In a bowl, a fruity pile,
One that makes me grin and smile.
A fuzzy orb with a flair,
It rolls away, oh it's a dare!

Slicing it brings out the giggles,
It squirts and splatters, oh how it wiggles.
Juice running wild, what a mess,
But let's be honest, I love the stress!

Spitting seeds like a champion ace,
It's truly a fruity fun race.
Each bite comes with a laugh or two,
Who knew snacks could be so askew?

So grab your napkin, wipe your chin,
This fruit fest is the greatest win.
With each bite, let the joy uncoil,
In the mess of laughs, we find our soil!

Nature's Sweet Lullaby

In the garden where the fruit grows,
A dance with bees and their little clothes.
The breeze tickles the leaves with glee,
While birds gossip about you and me.

Beneath the tree, a squirrel does twirl,
Chasing its tail, oh what a whirl!
Each giggle of nature, a playful tease,
Cozy whispers among the trees.

Golden Horizons of Summer Splendor

The sun spills juice across the sky,
While ants march on, oh my, oh my!
They think they're mighty, so bold and bright,
Gathering crumbs, they dance day and night.

With lemonade calls that chill the chest,
While we race to see who's the best.
In the splash of pools, we dive and pop,
Who knew summer could make us flip-flop?

Abundance in the Orchard's Heart

Orchard rows with fruits galore,
Like candy stores with nature's score.
We snack on nectar like royalty,
Chasing our laughter like a spree.

A raccoon sneaks in, he's looking sly,
With a wink, he snatches, oh my, oh my!
Nature's buffet, what a sight to crave,
We feast like kings, oh how we rave!

The Elixir of Warmth and Wonder

Sunshine bursts in a giggle so bright,
Splashing warmth, what a funny sight!
The clouds wear faces that grin and play,
As laughter echoes the whole day away.

A smoothie spill on a puppy's paw,
He shakes it off, what a comical flaw!
With every giggle and sprout all around,
Life's simple joys, in laughter, abound.

Sun's Laughter in Juicy Rapture

The sun giggles warmly, quite absurd,
As fruits wear their blush, it's mildly blurred.
Squirrels dance wildly, a nutty delight,
Chasing golden beams, from morning till night.

Sweet nectar drips from a careless grin,
Bumblebees buzz with a cheeky spin.
These ripened orbs bring chuckles and glee,
A feast for the eyes, as bright as can be.

Pies in the sky, clouds fluffy and round,
With laughter like bubbles, joy can be found.
Everyone smiles, their worries held tight,
In this crazy world, we savor the light.

So let's raise our cups with sticky sweet cheer,
For sunshine and laughter that draw ever near.
With each juicy burst and silly surprise,
We'll giggle together as summer complies.

The Velvet Caress of Juicy Bliss

Once upon a tree, so lavishly grand,
Fruits wield their colors, like bands of a band.
Each bite's a jest, a sweet trick for the tongue,
As giggles erupt, the laugh is quite sung.

Fuzzy and round, they tease the brave souls,
Daring us gently to give them our goals.
A playful ballet at the picnic's spread,
Where laughter erupts, like jelly on bread.

Juicy whispers float on the breeze,
Wandering like dreams, aiming to please.
Chasing the juice with a spoonful of fun,
Creating a mess, oh what have we done?

So summon the laughter, your slice of delight,
Embrace the soft velvet wrapped up tight.
With every sweet bite, the jokes come to play,
In this juicy circus, let's dance the day away.

Flickering Light on Blossom's Edge

In fields where flowers giggle and sway,
The blooms wear their laughter in bright disarray.
Ripened morsels hang like jokes in the air,
We pluck them with glee, without a care.

A firefly winks, lighting paths undefined,
To orchards of humor where joy's intertwined.
Carts of delight roll past with a grin,
In this carnival of flavor, let the fun begin!

Squirrels join in, with flamboyant flair,
Dressed in their nutty parade, do they dare?
Laughter's the theme in this zesty charade,
Beneath the bright whispers, a jubilant cascade.

So heed the sweet laughter that glimmers around,
In every soft moment, pure silliness found.
With a bounty like this, who could resist?
Join in the fun, let your worries desist!

Juicy Secrets of the Summer's Spine

A spine full of secrets, juicy and round,
Hides laughter and whispers beneath the ground.
Every fruit's giggle, ripe with surprise,
Makes summer a puzzle, where joy never dies.

Yeast of the season, bubbling and bold,
Harvests of chuckles, secrets untold.
Slices of sunshine, served with a twist,
Leap into joy, it's impossible to resist!

Frolicking shadows paint patterns so bright,
As laughter drips down like dew in the night.
Sipping on cheer, we gather and share,
These juicy delights come with festive flair.

So bring on the fun, let's gather in glee,
With smiles and stories, sweet serenity.
In every sweet moment, here's what we find,
Juicy secrets whispering, summer entwined.

Orchard Symphony

In an orchard full of cheer,
Tiny fruits dance, oh so near.
Squirrels jive, oh what a sight,
Mixing snacks 'til the stars are bright.

Bouncing round like a silly ball,
Juicy giggles, hear them all.
Wiggly worms join the parade,
In this fruity escapade!

Bees are buzzing a joyful tune,
As they bop beneath the moon.
Branches sway, a merry beat,
Who knew picking could be so sweet?

When the sun sets, they start to wail,
"Where's the pie? We need that trail!"
Laughter rings through every tree,
Funky fruits, happy as can be!

Luscious Dreams

Dreams of plums and apricots,
Dance in nap time's tangled knots.
Ripe and round, they tease my mind,
In puddles of nectar, joy I find.

Sticky fingers, sweetened bliss,
Each stolen bite a fruity kiss.
Giggling fruits play hide and seek,
In a grove so silly, cheek to cheek.

Cider streams and jelly flows,
Sugar-coated fun just grows.
Who needs a snack that's plain and bland?
When juicy jests can be so grand!

Wake me up to sunny sips,
With all these fruity friendships!
In dreams we gather, laugh and cheer,
For juicy joys are always near!

A Canvas of Flavor

On a canvas of vibrant hue,
Blobs of fruit paint a bright view.
Splashes of sweetness, colorful flair,
Creating giggles everywhere.

A squeeze of citrus, oh so bold,
Dripping fun, not just for gold.
Brush strokes of jelly and jam galore,
A masterpiece you can't ignore!

Lemonade rivers rush on by,
While strawberry suns light up the sky.
Rolling with laughter, shades of cream,
Life is just one big silly dream!

Tasting palettes, bright as day,
Capture giggles in each display.
Together we swirl in fruity cheer,
This canvas is fun, so let's all cheer!

Golden Gemstone

Golden gems on a gentle breeze,
Tickled by whispers from the trees.
Rolling around like bouncy toys,
Nature's sweet crunch brings us joys.

Toasting fruits in a sunny dance,
Giving life to each whimsical chance.
Chewing laughter with every bite,
Watch those giggles take flight!

A slice of sunshine, bright and round,
Transforming frowns into laughter sound.
Add a dash of silly fun,
Golden treasure for everyone!

As we munch, let's all sing,
Jubilant echoes, free as spring.
In the orchard, friendship's glee,
Golden gemstones, wild and free!

The Fruitful Haven

In a tree full of dreams, they sway here,
Juicy orbs of sweet laughter near.
Little hands reach high, giggles abound,
Fruits tumble down with a joyful sound.

A picnic spread wide, ants join the fun,
Wobbling, rolling, a race to be won.
Stick a fruit hat on a kid's head,
Laughter erupts, 'We're all fruit-fed!'

Squirrels jump in, with their chubby cheeks,
Snatching the treats, hear them squeak!
Nature's candy, oh so bright,
Every bite is pure delight!

Sunshine smiles down, what a sight,
Sticky fingers, faces full of light.
In the haven where we all play,
Fruity fun takes the day away!

Blissful Succulence

A juicy plunge into flavors divine,
Lemonade stories with each sip, we dine.
Laughter bubbles up, taste buds rejoice,
Fruits of the season, a reason to voice.

Sticky toes dance on the ground,
Sips and slips, here we are found.
Fruit hats bobbing, tip over wide,
"Catch the juice!" echoes our pride.

Contentment oozes from every bite,
Mirth and giggles in the warm twilight.
Splash in the pool, dive in with glee,
Fruity treasures shared among we.

Sundae surprises, a cherry on top,
Laughter erupts, spill not a drop!
Oh, the joy found in every seam,
In a rib-tickling, fruit-filled dream!

Sunkissed Delicacies

In the garden, sunlight's embrace,
Fruits twinkle, each in its place.
Bouncing berries, so plump and round,
Sticky fingers, joy unbound.

A toast to the day, hats of fruit wear,
Lemonade giggles burst in the air.
Wobbly tables with crumbs of cheer,
Where fruit and laughter draw us near.

Chasing shadows in playful retreat,
A fruity surprise at our little feast.
Throwing slices, then running away,
"Catch the essence!" we all play.

In the dusk, with moonlight's glow,
Berry dreams, we let them flow.
Our hearts are light, and spirits bright,
In the orchard's embrace, all feels just right!

Harvest Moon Reverie

Under the moon, the laughter swells,
Fruit-filled baskets, oh think of the smells!
Everyone munching with glee in delight,
This party gets crazier under the night.

Dancing around 'til the stars peek,
Fruit punch spills, we all squeak!
Lemon drops hidden, sugary gold,
Each bite tells a story, playful and bold.

Whispers of fruit tales come alive,
Crispy fun makes the night thrive.
Who knew harvest could be so bright?
We're the fruit ninjas, giving a fright!

As we gather, the laughter takes flight,
Sparkling moments under the moonlight.
Cheers to the flavors, the fun all around,
In this quirky garden, joy knows no bound!

Fables of Flavor

In a grove where fruits do dance,
A silly fruit will take a chance.
With wobbly steps, it starts to prance,
Inviting friends to join the trance.

A pear rolled by, quite out of line,
Said, "I'll join you in this rhyme!"
They giggled and they shared a bite,
Delightful chaos, pure delight!

An orange slipped, fell with a shout,
And all the fruits began to pout.
But laughter rang from tree to tree,
In this zany, fruity jamboree!

So gather round, enjoy the fun,
Where every fruit's a silly pun.
Forget the rule, just take a slice,
In this wild and wobbly paradise!

Sunshine's Offering

A sunbeam radiates a smile,
As fruits gather to share their style.
"I'm the juiciest!" cried out the lime,
"No way!" said berry, "I'm divine!"

A banana slipped on sunny beams,
And squished yourself to fruity dreams.
Grapes giggled as they rolled away,
In this sunshine-filled buffet!

They argued, tossed, and made a mess,
But laughter beat out the distress.
With every slip, they found their cheer,
Bellowing joy for all to hear!

So join the fruity fun today,
Where every shade brings bright hooray!
With sunshine's warmth and smiles in tow,
Silly fruit antics steal the show!

A Symphony of Savor

The fruits convene, a merry band,
Creating tunes that sway the land.
The mango played a vibrant beat,
While grapes danced light upon their feet.

Strawberry shook and twirled with flair,
While kiwi joined without a care.
The soundtrack grew, so free and clear,
As laughter mixed with fruity cheer!

A watermelon dropped its rhyme,
And caused a splatter in no time.
They laughed aloud, what a delight,
As juicy notes took joyful flight!

So sway and groove, among the trees,
Let flavors tease the summer breeze.
In harmony, they sing and sway,
This fruity symphony's here to play!

The Sunkissed Tapestry

In fields where sun and laughter meet,
Fruits weave a tapestry so sweet.
A swirled banana, bright and bold,
Wrapped up in stories yet untold.

With every twist and pop and cheer,
The fruits design a world sincere.
A pumpkin rolled in, round and jolly,
Join in the fun, it's quite a folly!

As apples giggle with delight,
Creating swirls both day and night.
The berries burst with color bright,
Painting joy in shades of light!

So come, indulge in fruity dreams,
Where silly laughter reigns in beams.
In this tapestry of sunlit grace,
Join the dance, and find your place!

Radiant Hues on Wistful Branches

Orange globes hang way up high,
Swaying gently in the sky.
A squirrel tries a daring leap,
Lands right where the juice will seep.

Birds below with twinkling eyes,
Watching for their fruity prize.
One swoops down, a fruity snack,
Misses it, and now it's back!

Bouncing bees buzz with a laugh,
Trying hard, they miss by half.
They dance around like silly clowns,
Covered in bright, sticky crowns.

Branches creak with giggles light,
While shadows play in sunny bright.
Ripening suns in evening glow,
Always brings a friend or so.

The Dance of Orchard Fairies

Fairies twirl in breezy space,
Whirling leaves, a fancy chase.
With wings that shimmer, bright and bold,
They sprinkle magic, tales untold.

A gnome trips over roots so sly,
As fairies laugh and flit on by.
They cast a spell with every giggle,
Make the blossoms dance and wiggle.

Laughter bubbles through the air,
As tiny sprites spin without care.
Fruit below starts to sway and shout,
"We want in on this fun, no doubt!"

Even shadows join the spree,
With goofy steps and jolly glee.
Underneath the twinkling lights,
They dance away into the nights.

Honeyed Days and Silken Nights

Morning sun with sticky flair,
Wakes the world from sleep's sweet snare.
Busy bees buzz, but watch out,
Someone is on a sugary route!

Wobbling squirrels, all in a line,
Chasing rays, it's snack time divine.
With a nut in paw, they miscalculate,
A tumble here, it's quite the fate!

Nights bring softness, dreams abound,
As sweet scents of fruit surround.
Moonlit treats on every tree,
As laughter fills the air with glee.

While crickets play a merry tune,
The stars join in, a sticky swoon.
Underneath the glimmering skies,
All find fun where sweetness lies.

Blossom and Bounty in the Breeze

Blossoms burst with colors bright,
Swinging on branches, what a sight!
Bouncers in the breeze do sway,
Whispers of joy lead the way.

Bouncing bunnies hop with cheer,
Through feathery clouds, they steer.
They nibble on what's sweet and fine,
While birds sing tunes in perfect line.

Frogs join in on the joyous song,
With splashes of fun, they bounce along.
Dancing in rhythm, what a display,
A gala of giggles, all night and day.

When dawn peeks in, a fresh surprise,
The bounty smiles, and laughter flies.
Every year brings forth a treat,
And every moment tastes so sweet.

Delights from the Grove

In the grove where fruits do laugh,
A fuzzy orb spills juice by half.
Dancers swoop and twirl around,
As sugar drips upon the ground.

With every bite, a giggle pops,
The laughter never, ever stops.
Stickiness adorns our joyful hands,
Like nature's sticky, happy bands.

Sunshine's glee and nectar's cheer,
A fruity feast that draws us near.
In this place, all worries fade,
As zesty jokes are deftly made.

So grab a nibble, take a seat,
Join the chorus, feel the beat.
With every smile and fruity glare,
Life's a treat we love to share.

Aromatic Whimsy

In fields where laughter meets the breeze,
A scent of sweetness, oh so tease!
The air's a stage, a funny show,
As giggles dance between the row.

A funky fruit sits, round and bright,
Winking at us with pure delight.
It slips and trips in playful jest,
Causing all to be quite a mess.

The bees buzz by, in suits of yellow,
They've come to join this fruity fellow.
With sticky feet and a zany spin,
In this whimsy, let the fun begin!

So take a whiff, embrace the cheer,
Let fruity frolics draw you near.
Nature's jokes in every sight,
Aromatic chuckles, pure delight!

Nature's Artistry

Nature's canvas holds its brush,
In orchards where the colors rush.
Like giggling goblins up a tree,
Creating art so wild and free.

With strokes of gold and dappled red,
A fruity smile, the joy we spread.
Each plump morsel sings a tune,
A funny ballet beneath the moon.

The squirrels prance with dainty flair,
Stealing bites without a care.
They dance around in sheer delight,
While we all laugh at their high flight.

So gather round this joyful sight,
Nature's jesters bring us light.
In every hue, a playful jest,
Artistry that feels the best.

Sweetness in Reverie

In dreams of tang and giggles bright,
Sweetness swirls in pure delight.
A fruity slice, a playful tease,
Floating softly on the breeze.

Happiness drips from every bite,
As the world spins with sheer delight.
Biting into blissful cheer,
With every taste, the laughter's near.

Moments sticky, yet so sweet,
Joking around on sugary feet.
In this reverie, joy outshines,
With every fruit, our laughter twines.

So let us feast on nature's joke,
Each slice a giggle, each sip we soak.
In sweetness found, our spirits lift,
A happy heart, the greatest gift.

Nectar Dreams in Orchard Shadows

In the grove where laughter grows,
Squirrels dance with fruit in toes.
A juicy bite, a slip, a slide,
Chasing dreams where sweetness hides.

A bee buzzed past, it wore a hat,
Sipping nectar, fancy that!
With every drop, a giggle spills,
In the shadows, joy instills.

Whispers float on summer's breeze,
As ants march by with chubby knees.
They stumble and play, oh what a sight,
In the orchard, hearts feel light.

So raise a toast to fruity fun,
With every laugh, we come undone.
In this land where humor sways,
Nectar dreams are here to stay.

Blushing Kiss of the Afternoon

In the sun where sweetness beams,
A giggle bursts like berry creams.
With every bite, a blush erupts,
As laughter's juice, our joy corrupts.

Silly squirrels with puffy cheeks,
Share their snacks and wink with freaks.
In this kiss of shining glow,
We chase the joy, just let it flow.

Posh chipmunks with tiny forks,
Eating fruit and pulling larks.
With every nibble, silly games,
And fruit-inspired funny names.

A sunny day, let's dance and sway,
In laughter's grip, we'll laugh and play.
Come join the feast, let's hear the cheer,
With each sweet nibble, we're still here!

Harvest of Sun-kissed Smiles

Oh what joy in golden light,
The harvest yields a funny sight.
With giggles bouncing on the breeze,
And silly dances that aim to please.

Bouncing fruits in playful race,
Chasing laughter, what a place!
A fruity crown upon our heads,
With sticky fingers, rumor spreads.

In the patch with laughter rife,
Competing with a grinning wife.
Each jest a splash of fruity cheer,
In every joke, the sun appears.

So stack those smiles up to the sky,
In this harvest, we all fly.
With every bite, our spirits glide,
In golden fields, let's share the ride.

Nectarine Serenade

Listen close, the fruits do sing,
Of funny tales that summers bring.
With every pluck, a giggle looms,
In orchards bright, we chase the blooms.

A family of ants in a grand parade,
Wobbling like they've all been played.
With nectar sweet, they strut and sway,
Inviting all to join the fray.

Chubby cheeks and sticky hands,
Spilling laughter, oh, it stands!
Each succulent morsel brings delight,
As funny moments spark the night.

So join the tune, a joyful ride,
In these sweet tales, we will confide.
With every laugh, we serenade,
In a world where fruits are made.

Sweet Flesh Beneath the Skin

Beneath a fuzzy coat, oh so fine,
Lies a treasure sweet, like sunshine.
Juices dribble down, quite the scene,
A funny feast, with giggles between.

Every bite a hiccup, laughter in air,
Sticky fingers and no time to spare.
With every munch, our worries depart,
Nature's candy, plays tricks on the heart.

Sunkissed cheeks, and grins all around,
With each juicy burst, joy is profound.
It's a comedic mess, but oh, what a treat,
We can't help but dance, to this fruity beat.

So here we are, in a fruity delight,
Fruits in our hair, what a silly sight.
A feast of joy, with laughter in sprawl,
In this sweet kingdom, we're having a ball.

Sunlit Whimsy in Every Bite

In the bright sun, they shine with flair,
A nibble brings giggles, no cause for despair.
With every sunny morsel, there's mischief to find,
Like sticky fingers, they play tricks on the mind.

They bounce on the trees, in bright playful hues,
Beneath sunlight's riddle, we can't refuse.
A chorus of chuckles fills the warm air,
Each bite like a giggle, without a care.

So here we munch, and the drama unfolds,
With bites full of whimsy, and stories retold.
It's a fruity frolic, a laughter parade,
With every fun bite, we're joyfully swayed.

Join in the revel, let smiles take flight,
In the sweet embrace of this sunny delight.
We sip on the juice, and dance 'til we're merry,
In this orchard of joy, where troubles seem scary.

Warm Embrace of the Orchard's Heart

In the orchard's heart, we find our glee,
With cozy hugs from every tree.
Each fruit a cuddle, a giggle to share,
The harvest brings joy, a sweet little affair.

Rolling in laughter, grass stains on knees,
A sticky affair, nature's tease.
Laughter erupts, with each fruity slip,
It's a slapstick moment, in every trip.

As the sun dips low, colors ignite,
We pop fruity gems, a tasty delight.
With each funny crunch, our giggles arise,
In the orchard's warmth, under twilight skies.

So let's all gather, in this warm embrace,
With fruits of laughter, we'll celebrate grace.
In this orchard, dear friends, we find our part,
Where each bite's a joy, and a chuckle will start.

Vibrant Hues in Twilight Glow

As twilight falls, the colors bloom,
Fruits painted bright, dispelling all gloom.
Biting into goodness, we can't stop the grin,
Each mouthful whispers, let the fun begin.

Under the moon, with laughter in waves,
Taste buds dance, as the sweetness behaves.
They burst with joy, like a joke gone right,
With every colorful pop, into the night.

So, grab a goblet of juice that flows,
Everyone twirls in laughter's throes.
With giggles and flavors, the evening takes flight,
In this vibrant glow, every moment feels light.

So gather around, as twilight unfolds,
The fruits are our songs, with stories retold.
In the night's warm embrace, we find our bliss,
In this fruity fun, live each giggly kiss.

Succulent Whispers

In a grove where fruits conspire,
Laughter bursts, we can't tire.
Juicy cheeks and sticky hands,
We play games with fruit demands.

Rolling balls down the path,
Juicing up with lots of laughs.
A fruit fight begins to spark,
With splashes bright, oh what a mark!

Friends abound with silly grins,
Wrestling juice, and slippery skins.
Sipping sweet from fragrant cups,
We giggle as the juice it slops.

In the end, we're soaked and bright,
But oh, what joy, what pure delight!
Our little orchard just a scene,
Of laughter rich and juicy sheen.

Elixir of the South

The sun is hot, the fruit is ripe,
A southern treat, our fun type.
With a wink and oh, a cheer,
We blend the nectar, bring it near.

Grab a cup, let's not be shy,
Fill it up, let spirits fly.
Swirling flavors dance with flair,
One sip, and we forget our care.

Wobble, giggle, spill a bit,
One more round, let's not quit!
The sweet parade forever sings,
Of summer bliss and all its things.

Laughter drips like the sugary flow,
Under the sun, our friendship grows.
A slapstick fight, a time to jest,
In this elixir, we find our best.

Dreams in a Fruit Bowl

In a bowl so round and bright,
Fruits tumbling, what a sight!
Bananas dance, and grapefruits sway,
A fruity show, come out and play.

Cherries giggle, apples grin,
A fruity party to begin!
Together they make quite the crew,
In sugary dreams, they break through.

Lemon twists with mad laughter,
Playing tag, fruit's happy ever after.
As the laughter fills the air,
Even veggies want to share!

In the end, a juicy feast,
A fruity joy, we're all released.
With every slice, the giggles swell,
In this bowl, we know it well.

Soft Beginnings

Morning light through the trees,
A fruit salad, oh, such a tease!
Sensations sweet, and colors bright,
Our adventure starts with a bite.

Sipping from a melon cup,
Smiles wide while we all sup.
Whipped cream clouds float above,
In this moment, we just love.

Fruits in hats, they strut around,
Silly shapes abound, profound!
With every chop and every slice,
We create a banquet, oh so nice!

As the sun climbs to the peak,
We serve up joy, no need to speak.
In this soft beginning's bliss,
Our laughter echoes, sealed with a kiss.

Orchard's Lullaby

In the orchard where they sway,
Chasing bees, they dance all day.
With a giggle, watch them roll,
Plump and juicy, heart and soul.

Squirrels giggle in the trees,
Hiding snacks with such a tease.
They tumble down with silly grace,
A fruity frenzy, what a race!

Ripe treasures buried deep in leaves,
Napping under sunlit eaves.
A bloom of color, laughter spills,
Nature's jokes, all good-natured thrills.

Underneath the moonlit sky,
Fruit flies buzz and softly sigh.
This orchard's tune, a blissful sound,
In every bite, pure joy is found.

Ripe with Joy

In the grove where laughter grows,
Crispy crunches, sweet repose.
Gather 'round, let's munch away,
Let those giggles rule the day!

Fruits are swinging, oh what fun,
Bouncing like a playful bun.
Juicy dribbles, sticky hands,
Hilarity in fruity bands.

With a wink, a juicy fling,
Chasing down the silly spring.
Berry stains and laughter loud,
Join the merry, hungry crowd!

Each bite a burst, a chuckle's cheer,
A feast of fun, come join us here!
With every slice, our joy's displayed,
In this taste parade, we've made.

Fragrant Fantasia

In a world of swirling scents,
Fruity jokes and playful hints.
Smiles as sweet as summer sun,
Fruit salad's a frolicsome run!

Banana giggles, a laughing pear,
A funny face, we all can share.
Kiwi's whispers, a giggly charm,
Tickling taste buds, safe from harm.

Cherries chat with their glossy hats,
Banter floats with giggles and spats.
In this garden, laughter blooms,
Silly fruit, the joy resumes!

With a twist, we tumble and roll,
In this fantasy, we find our goal.
Every bite, a jester's cheer,
A fruity dream, oh come, my dear!

Sunbeam Slices

Slices basking in sunlight's glow,
Golden laughter begins to flow.
Each bite a sunny, giggly ray,
Bringing joy to every day!

Lemons chuckle with a zesty tease,
Mango mischief flutters with ease.
Berries bounce, catching the breeze,
In this orchard, we find our keys!

A fruit parade with sparkles bright,
Silly antics, pure delight.
With juicy smiles, we dance around,
On this fruity merry-go-round!

Generous slices, serve them quick,
In a fruity flick, we take our pick.
With laughter tangled in every zest,
In this sunlit slice, we're truly blessed!

The Tender Fruit

In the orchard, fruits abound,
They giggle and dance on the ground.
A drop of juice, a sticky spree,
Oh, my shirt, it won't come free!

With every bite, a burst of cheer,
Squishy sweetness, oh so dear.
I shared my snack with a cheeky bee,
Now he thinks he's part of me!

In toppings, salads, pies galore,
Each slice, a smile that we adore.
But watch out where those pits reside,
One wrong crunch, oops! I just cried!

So here's to fruits that make us grin,
With laughter and juice, let's dive in.
Life's too short for sorrow or pout,
So come on now, let's play it out!

Heart of Fuzz

Oh fuzzy orb with a sunny face,
You roll into the strangest place.
With all your fluff and sweet perfume,
You raised a joy, a fruit-filled boom!

I spy a fruit bowl growing bold,
Each peachy gem, a story told.
But sometimes they play a sneaky game,
Leaving pit surprises, that's real lame!

At picnics, they're the star of the day,
With ice cream or just on display.
But watch your step on the sunny grass,
You might just slip, oh what a pass!

Every bite is a burst of fun,
Rolling laughter like a run.
So grab a fruit and toss it high,
Catch it quick, and give a try!

Sun-drenched Delights

In sunshine's warmth, fruits shine so bright,
Wobbly treats that give pure delight.
A wink from a peach, a grin from a pear,
Their juicy whispers float in the air.

Underneath the tree, we share a snack,
With little giggles, no turning back.
Faces all sticky, laughter in air,
What's that smell? Oh wait, it's hair!

Summer days bring fun aplenty,
Sticky hands turn all things trendy.
We toss our seeds, they fly like dreams,
Splat on a head? Oh, giggles and screams!

So grab a fruit in all its glory,
Let's spin this tale and write our story.
For every bite we share and laugh,
Is a joyful dance, our fruity path!

Nectar of Joy

Sweet nectar drips from golden skin,
In every bite, the joy begins.
With slurps and giggles all around,
We savor flavors that astound!

Imagining a grand fruit band,
With plucky beats from every hand.
They strum and sway, we bop along,
To the rhythm of our fruity song!

In every bite, a burst of laughter,
Moments that we chase after.
Who knew you'd bring us all such glee,
Oh, fuzzy fellow, you and me!

So raise a cup, let's toast to cheer,
For every fruit who brings us near.
With joyful hearts, we munch away,
And dance like it's the best of days!

Sweet Amber Memories

In the orchard, laughter swells,
Fruits collide, as nature yells.
Juicy drips on summer cheeks,
Tickling taste buds, joy it seeks.

Squirrels dance with mischievous flair,
Stealing snacks without a care.
Pies are baked with love and cheer,
Chasing away our every fear.

Sticky fingers, messy shirts,
Wiping faces, oh how it hurts!
Moments shared with silly grins,
Countless games, let the fun begin!

Each bite brings a funny tale,
Of runaway fruits and sweetened trails.
In every slice, a giggle hides,
As laughter and sweetness collide.

The Allure of Ripeness

The clock strikes noon, the sun is bold,
A playful scent, stories unfold.
Round and plump, the treasures gleam,
In fields of gold, they reign supreme.

With every taste, a giggle grows,
A wild dance where flavor flows.
Swirling juices, oh what fun!
Catch the mess before it runs!

Golden nectar drips like rain,
While bees hum sweetly, never plain.
A tug-of-war in sticky games,
All in the name of fruity claims.

In the breeze, it's pure delight,
Laughter echoes, day turns night.
Out in the sun, the fun don't stop,
With every bite, we're on the top!

Tangy Drizzles

A splash of zest, a twirl of cream,
Slippery treats, oh how they gleam!
Daring spoons dive into the bowl,
Drizzles dance, taking their toll.

Sour notes with sugar sweet,
A flavor war, oh what a feat!
Lemons laugh, and berries pout,
But together, they sing out loud.

Silly spills on the table spread,
Chasing crumbs like things we dread.
Tickled tongues and smirking eyes,
It's a party beneath the skies!

From drizzle drop to messy grin,
In fruity chaos, we always win.
Each tangy twist, a joyful rhyme,
Laughter echoes, one taste at a time.

Warmth in Every Bite

Ovens warm, with smiles inside,
Baking dreams on a funky ride.
Crusty shells, a golden hue,
Filling dreams for me and you.

With every slice, a quirky laugh,
Melted goo, a silly craft.
Chasing crumbs from plate to face,
Each flavor holds a funny race.

Nuts and spice, oh what a mix!
Tickling tongues with playful tricks.
Who can share just one small bite?
In each morsel, pure delight!

Warmth surrounds, a happy flare,
Laughter echoes, dances in air.
With every joke, and silly fight,
We find joy in every bite.

Fruity Whispers of Summer

In gardens bright, they giggle loud,
Little fruits, they form a crowd.
Wobbling on branches, a comical sight,
They dance in the breeze, full of delight.

Juicy giggles, laughter fills the air,
Buzzing bees join in, without a care.
Every fruit has a tale to tell,
Of sunlit fun, oh, quite a swell!

Lemon's sour face wears a big grin,
While cherries play tag, trying to win.
In this fruity fair, the jokes unwind,
A fruit salad of laughs, truly one of a kind.

Summer's stage, where, under the sun,
Every juicy character loves to run.
With a wink and a jig, they steal the show,
Whispers of laughter in the sun's warm glow.

Juicy Breezes and Velvet Skies

A breeze blows softly, spinning delight,
Fruits tumble down, it's quite a sight!
Bananas slip, with a funny slosh,
While grapefruits giggle in a juicy posh.

Velvet skies above, with clouds like cream,
Oranges drift, they begin to gleam.
Rolling down hills with a citrusy cheer,
They shout to the world, 'We're fruity and here!'

Every bite bursts with giggles and grins,
When apples tell stories of wild spins.
Let's sip on sunshine, let joy be our guide,
In this silly orchard, we'll laugh till we cried.

A fruit parade marches right down the lane,
With berries dancing, who's counting the rain?
Juicy breezes, soft laughter, oh my!
Where fruity fun under velvet skies flies.

The Sweetness of Sun-drenched Mornings

Bright orange sun spills laughter wide,
Each fruity friend takes a jovial ride.
Mornings drizzled with nectar so sweet,
Dance of flavors, a fruity treat!

Pineapple in shades, wears its crown just right,
While strawberries giggle, causing a fright.
Twirling around, they jump, they play,
In the warmth, they frolic, all through the day.

Melon slices, with bright, silly grins,
Share their secrets of giggly sins.
"Let's roll down the hill, we'll make quite a splash!"
Under the sun, in a fruit-filled bash!

Every morning's a canvas, painted with joy,
Where laughter's the music, every girl and boy.
In a bowl of sunshine, let's mix and blend,
The sweetness of mornings, where fun won't end.

Golden Orbs of Sunlit Joy

Golden orbs, hanging by the vines,
Spinning tales of fruity designs.
Lemonade laughter spills on the ground,
As citrusy cheer in the air is found.

A peach with a wink and a radish in tow,
Tells jokes of the garden in a vibrant show.
'What did the berry say to the cherry?'
'Let's make a smoothie—sounds rather merry!'

Under the sunshine, they tumble with glee,
Bananas unite for a fruity jamboree.
Cheeky coconuts shout, "Join us, don't wait!"
In this golden realm, we celebrate fate!

So gather around, let laughter ignite,
In fields of flavor, with joy so bright.
Golden orbs of happiness, spinning and swirlin',
In the heart of summer, laughter's unfurlin'.

Silken Tones in Sunset's Glow

In fields where colors swirl and dance,
Fruits giggle in a sunlit trance.
A fuzzy peach drops with a grin,
Saying, "Catch me, let the fun begin!"

Bouncing from branches, cheers arise,
Nature's laughter, oh what a surprise!
Juicy dribbles, sweet as a song,
Who knew that fruits could play along?

Sticky fingers, laughter in the air,
The silly antics, no one can compare.
Sit and munch, our worries out flown,
Who knew this fruit could steal the show?

So let's toast to the silliness we find,
In the golden glow, oh so kind.
With every bite, joy on the go,
Nature's humor in each sweet glow.

Harvesting Whimsy from Nature's Hand.

Underneath the sprawling tree,
Whimsical fruits tease, full of glee.
Wobbling on branches, they peek out,
"Pick me first!" they giggle and shout.

A basket ready, oh what a sight,
But the fruits have chosen to take flight!
They roll and tumble, a joyful parade,
Nature's jesters, lively and played.

Slip on skins and laugh we do,
As fuzzy curves take flight and flew.
Raspberry red and sunshine gold,
With every twist, a tale unfolds.

Savor the sweetness, let's play more,
Life's too short to only adore.
Grab your friends, come join the fun,
In nature's harvest, we're all one.

Fuzzy Embrace

In a land where giggles reign,
Fruits wear fuzz like a champ, it's plain.
With each bite, we laugh and sigh,
Giving our taste buds a joy to fly.

Round and plump, they tease and jest,
"Who's picking now?" they jest with zest.
Roll in the basket, a merry chase,
Nature's hugs, we embrace with grace.

Toasty sunbeams, a fruity hug,
Sipping sweet juice, feeling snug.
Their laughter echoes, in every bite,
Turned to giggles, a sheer delight.

Fuzzy companions, come join our cheer,
With nature's joy, let's smooch and steer.
Beneath the boughs, the fun will last,
In every moment, a friendship vast.

Orchard Whispers

In the orchard where secrets flow,
Fruits in huddles, whisper and glow.
"Tell me your tales!" they chime with cheer,
Forgotten stories we yearn to hear.

Sneaky squirrels join in the spree,
Nibbling on bites, as bold as can be.
Laughter bubbles in the summer air,
With each juiced smile, they banter and share.

Branches sway as if to tease,
"Dance with us in the gentle breeze!"
Rolling and bouncing, a zesty show,
In these orchard whispers, we all know.

So gather 'round, dear friends of mine,
Join the fun in this fruity shrine.
With every giggle, the world feels right,
In the orchard's whispers, our hearts take flight.

Biting into Sunshine

In the garden, laughs abound,
Bright orbs of joy roll on the ground.
I took a bite, oh what a treat,
Juicy squirt, a sticky feat!

Laughter echoes, juice does fly,
Squeezing fruit, oh me, oh my!
On my shirt, a sunny stain,
Sweet reminders, no shame, no pain.

Friends all gather, smiles so wide,
Each bite brings a joyful ride.
Who knew fruit could be so fun?
Chasing children, on the run!

So we munch with glee and cheer,
Nature's candy brings us near.
Laughter's the best, you'll agree,
In our fruity jubilee!

The Sweetest Indulgence

A fruit so round, I cannot wait,
To nibble on this tasty fate.
Crisp and sweet, a surefire win,
One juicy bite, let the fun begin!

Hoarding treasures, one by one,
Eat it fast, or it will run!
Giggles spill, like juice from skin,
Sweet sticky joy, let the day spin!

Of all the things that make me grin,
This little sphere holds joy within.
The sweetness dances, oh so bright,
Every bite's a pure delight!

With friends around, the laughter flows,
No time for woes, just fruity shows.
Together, we revel, cheers abound,
In this sweet bliss, joy is found!

Tales from the Orchard

Whispers in the trees today,
Fruits are plotting, come what may.
Happy squirrels, they scamper near,
The tales they tell fill us with cheer!

A wobbly branch, a sudden slip,
Down it rolls, a daring trip!
We all laugh till our bellies ache,
As juicy wonders start to shake.

The orchard's secrets, oh so sweet,
Laughter rises with each treat.
Beneath blue skies, we spin and sway,
Gathering joy in the warm sun's ray.

Every bite, a story shared,
Crisp and cheerful—no one's scared.
In this fruit-filled merry land,
We play and eat, hand in hand!

Juicy Dawn

Morning rays and colors flare,
Nature wakes without a care.
I spy a fruit that calls my name,
With every bite, I play the game!

Dancing dew on luscious skin,
A little chuckle, let the fun begin!
Biting in, oh such a splash,
Followed by laughter in a dash.

Sunshine tickles, taste starts to bloom,
In my mouth, a fruity swoon.
Chasing friends, a joyful spree,
This happy morning, just fruit and me!

With every munch, the day feels bright,
Our giggles echo, pure delight.
So here's to dawn, so juicy, sweet,
Life's funny moments, a real treat!

Luscious Landings

In a world where fruit does bounce,
Lemon's hat becomes the crown.
Melons roll and wiggle free,
Bouncing high with glee like me.

Pineapples dance in grass so bright,
Shaking hips with all their might.
Cherries giggle with their friends,
Making laughter that never ends.

Kiwis wearing tiny shoes,
Caper on as if to choose.
Tropical beats make them sway,
Every fruit's a party today.

Finally, figs start to tease,
Whispering secrets to the breeze.
Join the fun, let's not delay,
In this realm where fruits will play.

Whispers of Juiciness

A grape slipped on a juicy floor,
Flopped around, then asked for more.
With every bump, it waved its hands,
Joining up with other fruit bands.

Bananas in a silly race,
Slipping past at lightning pace.
They giggle, tumble, lose their place,
Rolling round in fruity grace.

Strawberries held a secret chat,
About the best way to sit flat.
They brewed up smoothies in a pot,
While oranges cheered, "Give it a shot!"

With a splash, the juice erupts,
Tickling noses, fruit erupts.
Laughter echoes in the sun,
In a world where fruit's all fun!

A Rhapsody of Fruit

In the garden where the spotlights glow,
Fruits audition for a show.
Apples juggling, pears on skates,
Making sure it's never late.

Berries join with a burst of song,
Singing loud, they can't go wrong.
Melodies mixed with bursts of zest,
This fruity choir is at its best.

An avocado, shy and smooth,
Makes a mess, begins to groove.
Dancing chips, they join the vibe,
Salsa moves, can't say the scribe.

As nighttime falls, they tell tall tales,
Of juicy journeys and fruity flails.
In this symphony of delight,
Laughter spins beneath the moonlight.

Fields of Gold

In a field where lemons shine,
Giggling sloths think it's divine.
Coconuts roll in with flair,
Swinging low just like a pair.

Peppers pink and oddly shaped,
Join the fun in their silly capes.
Whirling 'round like tiny stars,
Making friends from lands afar.

Straw hats worn by cantaloupes,
Crafting loud and fruity hopes.
They twirl and spin until they drop,
Creating a funny fruity bop.

With nightfall comes a tasty treat,
Pie contests for all to eat.
In the fields where giggles rise,
Everything is a fun surprise!

Lush Fruit Fantasies

In a garden where laughter grows,
Chubby cheeks and silly toes.
Fruits wearing crowns of bright hues,
Tickle my funny bone, what a muse!

Giggling berries dance in the sun,
Mangoes whisper, 'Let's have some fun!'
Bananas slip with laughter loud,
Waving to a cheerful crowd.

A fruit parade with silly hats,
Where oranges chase down playful cats.
Cherry giggles on the tree,
Join the fun, come laugh with me!

So come and feast, it's all a joke,
Jellybeans and giggles, no need to poke.
Grab a slice, let's share a laugh,
In this fruity world, we'll take a gaffe!

Sun-Kissed Bliss

Sunbeams dance on plump, round spheres,
Fruitful laughs chase away all fears.
A jolly lemon cracks a grin,
Sour-faced grapes, let the giggles begin.

Wobbly melons roll around,
Jolly laughter is the sweetest sound.
Plucking cherries from the trees,
Tasting silliness with the breeze.

Juicy jokes wrapped in a rind,
Goodness me, they're one of a kind!
An apple's pun gets everyone snickering,
It's a riot of flavors, just fickering.

Bring your friends, let's slice and cheer,
Turn the fruit bowl into a sphere.
With each mouthful, let's not resist,
For in this bliss, there's humor kissed!

The Velvet Dawn

As dawn breaks, the fruits awake,
Laughter ripples like a lake.
Smooth as velvet, bright and bold,
Sweet secret jokes just waiting to be told.

Strawberries wear their best attire,
Cackling as they bask in the fire.
Ripe and ready, they shine so bright,
Chasing off shadows with pure delight.

Cantaloupes giggle, hiding their face,
In this fruity world, there's always space.
Bananas stand proud, doing the hula,
While sleepy pears become a bit cooler.

So join this fun at sunrise's start,
Let fruity jokes fill your heart.
With every bite, a laugh will rise,
In this velvet dawn, humor never dies!

Honeyed Hues

Golden fruits with smiles so wide,
Fuzzy skins, they take great pride.
Lemonade giggles, sweet and bright,
In this honeyed realm, everything's light.

Bumbling bees dance round the blooms,
Learning comedy from fruity looms.
With each buzz, there's a punchline near,
It's a ticklish world, spread the cheer!

Peppers blush and the grapes all roar,
Telling tales of juicy folklore.
The jolly figs wear party hats,
Serving laughter alongside their chats.

So take a sip, let's have a blast,
In this rainbow of flavors, nothing can last.
With honeyed hues, let's toast and play,
In every fruit, there's joy on display!

Goosebumps of Summer

Warm sunbeams play, bright as can be,
Splashing in pools, we giggle with glee.
Sticky fingers, ice cream in hand,
Nature's confetti, so sweetly planned.

Bumblebees buzzing a happy old tune,
Tickling our noses, they dance 'round at noon.
We wear flowers, like crowns on our heads,
Making up stories in hammocky beds.

Flip-flops are flying, and laughter's in air,
Chasing our shadows without a care.
Once in a while, we trip on our feet,
Pirouettes turning to clumsy defeat.

But who really minds? The sun is our friend,
We savor each moment, let time twist and bend.
So here's to the summer, filled with delight,
Life's silly shenanigans, always in sight.

Fragrance of the Orchard

Swinging on branches, we reach for the sky,
Competition's fierce, who can pick high?
Juicy treasures just beyond reach,
What happened to wisdom? Oh, what a breach!

Robins are chirping, they laugh at our games,
As we pluck shiny jewels, calling them names.
"Smelly pink orbs!" one friend guffaws,
"It's fruit, not a monster!" shouts back with applause.

Fumbling and tumbling through fragrant delight,
Trying to catch bees with all of our might.
Instead, we catch laughter that soon fills the air,
Shouting, "Watch out! There's a bug in my hair!"

The orchard's alive with our festival sounds,
Giggles and wiggles, no one's safe from bounds.
As long as there's fun, we'll have a grand feast,
Taking silly snapshots, say cheese—at least!

Lush Labyrinth

Winding paths in greenery lush,
We wander aimlessly, there's no need to rush.
Bouncing around like a bouncy ball,
"Found my way home!" Wait, not at all!

We're lost in a sea of tall, wavy grass,
Sneaking up softly to give squirrels some sass.
Twisting and turning with giggles and grins,
Who knew getting lost could lead to such wins?

Trail of breadcrumbs? More like candy canes,
Follow the giggles, ignore all the pains.
"Who needs a map when you have silly friends?"
Around every corner, our lunacy bends.

So here in the maze, we banter and shout,
Share silly secrets, the kind that make doubt.
Each turn brings treasure, in jocular cheer,
Living our days, full of giggles and beer!

Slices of Bliss

Round, golden circles, so juicy and bright,
Each slice a treasure, a pure, tasty bite.
"Who wants some?" we cry with a goofy, big grin,
We snatch at the flavors, let the feast begin!

Seeds go a-flying, we giggle and chat,
"Oops, that one landed on Grandma's old cat!"
Wearing our snacks, like a sticky crown,
Making sure laughter is never shut down.

Flavors of sunshine dance on our tongues,
Delicious and messy, we sing silly songs.
Getting all tangled in juice and delight,
"Pass me a napkin!" is never polite.

So here's to the slices, the bursts and the fun,
We savor each moment, 'til days are all done.
When life hands you fruit, don't you hesitate,
Join in on the revelry; it's never too late!

www.ingramcontent.com/pod-product-compliance
Lightning Source LLC
Chambersburg PA
CBHW060121230426
43661CB00003B/279